THE
CALVARY
ROAD

By the same author:

THE CALVARY ROAD

ROY HESSION

With added notes by **Lynn Green**
Regional Director, YWAM

*If any man would come after me, he must
deny himself and take up his cross daily
and follow me." (Luke 9:23).*

Alresford, Hants SO24 9BJ
England

Originally published 1950
Copyright © CLC
51 The Dean, Alresford, Hampshire SO24 9BJ
Seventeenth Printing 1978
Combined edition with *Be Filled Now*
Printed in 1988

This revised edition 1995
Copyright © CLC
Reprinted 2003

ISBN 0 900284 67 6

Conception, Design and Production
Copyright © Gazelle Creative 1995.

Added notes Copyright © 1995 Lynn Green
Youth With A Mission, Ambrose Lane,
Harpenden, Herts AL5 4BX.

Scripture quotations unless otherwise noted are taken
from the New International Version © 1973, 1978,
1984 International Bible Society.

Road photo: Alison Hickey

Designed and Produced in England for CLC
51 The Dean, Alresford, Hampshire SO24 9BJ by
Gazelle Creative Productions Ltd, Concorde House,
Grenville Place, Mill Hill, London NW7 3SA.

Contents

Contents

Foreword

George Verwer
OM International

I believe that *The Calvary Road* is one of the most important and strategic books in the history of the church.

Hundreds and thousands of copies have gone around the globe in dozens of languages. I had the joy of having a close friendship with Roy Hession and saw him put his message into practice.

I believe this message is as relevant as ever in this new millennium. It will take only a few hours to read, but can lead to a lifetime of victory, power and reality. It is good to read it slowly and devotionally. Please be sure to get some extra copies and pass them on to others. When you get to glory, you will discover the amazing results.

George Verwer

Introduction

T*he Calvary Road* was first published in
February 1950. With the passage of years
I am more than ever sure that the truths
expressed in *The Calvary Road*, lie at the heart
of all those movements of revival by which
God has restored His Church to new life in the
hours of her dryness and need. Such
movements of revival are not only glorious
memories of the past, but are taking place right
now in various parts of the world. The
outward forms of such revivals do, of course,
differ considerably but the inward and
permanent content of them all is always the
same — a new experience of conviction of sin;
a new vision of the Cross of Jesus and of
redemption; a new willingness for brokenness,
repentance, confession and restitution; a joyful
experience of the power of the blood of Jesus
to cleanse fully from sin and restore and heal
all that sin has lost and broken; a new entering
into the fullness of the Holy Spirit and of His

power to do His own work through His people; and a new gathering in of the lost to Jesus. Inasmuch as this is what is happening now in various parts of the world, these pages have a special relevance for the reader today and I trust may, by the blessing of God, be the means of helping many to come to the Cross and present themselves as candidates for revival by the confession of their emptiness and failure.

Edited from Roy Hession's Foreword,
January 1988

1
BROKENNESS

We want to be very simple in this matter of revival. Revival is the life of the Lord Jesus poured into human hearts. Jesus is always victorious. In heaven they praise Him continually for His victory. Whatever may be our experience of failure and barrenness, He is never defeated. His power is boundless. We, on our part, have only to get into a right relationship with Him. Then we shall see His power being demonstrated in our hearts and lives and service, and His victorious life will fill us and overflow through us to others. That is the essence of revival.

If, however, we are to come into this right relationship with Him, the first thing we must learn is that our will must be broken to His will. To be broken is the beginning of revival. It is painful, it is humiliating, but it is the only way. It is being 'Not *I*, but *Christ*',[1] and a '*C*' is a bent '*I*'. The Lord Jesus cannot live in us fully and reveal Himself through us until the

proud self within us is broken. This simply
means that the hard, unyielding self, which
justifies itself, wants its own way, stands up for
its rights, and seeks its own glory, at last bows
its head to God's will, admits that it is wrong,
gives up its own way to Jesus, surrenders its
rights, and discards its own glory in order that
the Lord Jesus might have all and be all. In
other words, it is dying to self and
self-attitudes.

As we look honestly at our Christian lives,
we can see how much of this self there is in
each of us. It is so often self who tries to live
the Christian life (the mere fact that we use the
word 'try' indicates that it is self who has the
responsibility). It is self, too, who is often
engaged in Christian work. It is always self
who gets irritable, envious, resentful, critical and
worried. It is self who is hard and unyielding in
its attitude to others. It is self who is shy,
self-conscious and reserved. No wonder we
need breaking. As long as self is in control,
God can do little with us, for the fruit of the
Spirit (see Galatians 5), with which God longs
to fill us, is the complete opposite of the hard,
unbroken spirit within us and presupposes that
self has been crucified.

Being broken is both God's work, and ours.
He brings His pressure to bear, but we have to
make the choice. If we are really open to
conviction as we seek fellowship with God, He
will show us the expressions of this proud,
hard self that cause Him pain. At this point
we can either stiffen our necks and refuse to

repent, or we can bow our heads and say, 'Yes,
Lord.' Brokenness in daily experience is
simply a humble response to the conviction of
God. Inasmuch as this conviction is
continuous, we shall need to be broken
continually. This can be very costly when we
see all that this will involve — the rights and
selfish interests that will need to be given up
and the confessions and restitutions that may
also be necessary.

For this reason, we are not likely to be
broken except at the Cross of Jesus. The
willingness of Jesus to be broken for us is the
all-compelling motive for us to be broken too.
We see Him, who is in the form of God,
counting not equality with God a prize to be
grasped at and hung on to, but letting it go for
us and taking upon Himself the form of a
servant — God's servant, man's servant. We
see Him willing to have no rights of His own,
no home of His own, no possessions of His
own, willing for men to hurl their insults at
Him and not retaliate, willing to let men tread
on Him and not strike back or defend Himself.
Above all, we see Him broken as He meekly
goes to Calvary to become men's scapegoat by
bearing their sins in His own body on the tree.
In a prophetic psalm, He says, 'I am a worm
and not a man'.[2] Those who have been in
tropical lands tell us that there is a big
difference between a snake and a worm when
you attempt to strike at them. The snake rears
itself up, hisses, and tries to strike back — a
true picture of self. But a worm offers no

resistance, it allows you to do what you like with it, kick it or squash it under your heel — a picture of true brokenness. Jesus was willing to become just that for us — a worm and not a man. He did so, because that is what He saw us to be, worms having forfeited all rights by our sin, except the right to hell. He now calls us to take our rightful place as worms for Him and with Him. The whole Sermon on the Mount, with its teaching of non-retaliation, love for enemies and selfless giving, assumes that that is our position. But only the vision of the love that was willing to be broken for us can compel us to be willing for that to happen.

> Lord, bend that proud and stiff-necked I,
> Help me to bow the head and die;
> Beholding Him on Calvary,
> Who bowed His head for me.

But dying to self is not a thing we do once and for all. There may be an initial dying when God first shows these things. After that it will be a constant dying, for only in this way can the Lord Jesus be revealed constantly through us.[3] All day long the choice will be before us in a thousand ways. It will mean no plans, no time, no money, no pleasure of our own. It will mean constantly yielding to those around us; the true measure of how much we are yielded to God. Every humiliation, everyone who tries and annoys us, is God's way of breaking us, so that there is an even deeper channel for the life of Christ to flow in us.

You see, the only life that pleases God, and the only one that can be victorious, is His life — never our life, no matter how hard we try. But inasmuch as our self-centred life is the exact opposite of His, we can never be filled with His life, unless we are prepared for God to bring our life constantly to death. And in that we must co-operate by our moral choice.

Notes
1. Galatians 2:20   2. Psalm 22:6   3. 2 Corinthians 4:10.

To Think About

The apostle Paul lived and wrote about the life of brokenness. In 1 Corinthians 15:31 he wrote, "I die every day." And in Ephesians 4:22,23 he wrote, "put off your old self...be made new in the attitude of your mind." This is not a distant theological concept or a process which occurs without my active participation. It is my response to God's conviction and it is usually painful, but always worth that pain.

Am I walking in brokenness today — right now?

Have I heard God's convicting voice today? Did I respond by confessing to Him and, where appropriate, to others?

Personal notes

_____

_____

_____

_____

_____

_____

2

CUPS RUNNING OVER

Brokenness, however, is but the beginning of revival. Revival itself is being completely filled to overflowing with the Holy Spirit, and that is victorious living. If we were asked this moment if we were filled with the Holy Spirit, how many of us would dare answer 'Yes'? Revival is when we can say 'yes' at any moment of the day. It is not boastful to say so, for filling to overflowing is totally and completely God's work — it is all grace. All we have to do is to present our empty, broken self and let Him fill us and keep us filled. Andrew Murray says, 'Just as water ever seeks and fills the lowest place, so the moment God finds you abased and empty, His glory and power flow in.' The picture that has made things simple and clear for many of us is that of the human heart as a cup which we hold out to Jesus, longing that He may fill it with the water of life. Jesus is pictured carrying the golden water-pot with the water of life. As He passes by, He looks into our cup, and if it is clean He fills it to overflowing with the water of life. As Jesus is always passing by, the cup can be always running over. This is something of what David meant when he said, 'My cup overflows'. This is revival — the constant peace of God ruling in our hearts because we are full to overflowing with blessing, both for ourselves and for others. People imagine that dying to self makes us miserable, but it is just the opposite. It is the refusal to die to self that makes us miserable. The more we know of death with Him, the more we shall know of His life in us, and so know more of real peace and joy. His life, too, will overflow through us to lost souls in a real concern for their salvation, and to our fellow Christians in a deep desire for their blessing.

Under the blood

Only one thing prevents Jesus filling our cups as He passes by, and that is sin in one of its thousand forms. The Lord Jesus does not fill dirty cups. Anything that springs from self, however small, is sin. Self-effort or self-complacency in service is sin. Self-pity in trials or difficulties, self-seeking in business or Christian work, self-indulgence in one's spare time; all these are sin. Sensitiveness, touchiness, resentment, and self-defence when we are hurt or injured by others, self-consciousness, reserve, worry, fear, all spring from self and all are sin and make our

cups unclean.[1] But all of them were put into
that other cup, which the Lord Jesus shrank
from momentarily in Gethsemane, but which
he drank to the dregs at Calvary — the cup of
our sin. If we will allow Him to show us what
is in our cups and then give it to Him, He will
cleanse our cups in the precious blood that still
flows for sin. That does not mean cleansing
merely from the guilt of sin, but also from the
stain and pollution of it, so that we have 'no
more knowledge of sin'. And as He cleanses
our cups, so He fills them to overflowing with
His Holy Spirit. And each day we are able to
avail ourselves of that precious blood.
Suppose you have allowed the Lord Jesus to
cleanse your cup and have trusted Him to fill it
to overflowing, then something comes along
— a touch of envy or temper. What happens?
Your cup becomes dirty and it ceases to
overflow. If we are constantly being defeated
in this way, then our cup never overflows.

   If we are to know continuous revival we
must learn how to keep our cups clean. It is
never God's will that a revival should cease
and be known in history as the revival of this
year or that year. When that happens it is due
to one thing only — sin, those little sins that
the devil drops into our cup. But if we go
back to Calvary and learn again the power of
the blood of Jesus to cleanse moment by
moment from the beginnings of sin, then we
have learnt the secret of cups constantly
cleansed and constantly overflowing. The
moment you are conscious of that touch of

envy, criticism, irritability, whatever it is —
give it to Jesus and ask Him to wash it away
by the power of His blood. You will find the
reaction gone, your joy and peace restored,
and your cup running over. The more you
come for cleansing in this way, the less you will
have these reactions. But cleansing is possible
only when we have first been broken before
God on the point concerned. Suppose we are
irritated by certain traits in someone. It is not
enough to take our reactions of irritation to
Calvary.

We must first be broken, that is, we must
yield to God over the whole question, and
accept that person and their ways as His will
for us. Then we are able to take our wrong
reaction to Jesus, knowing that His blood will
wash away our sin. When we have been
cleansed from sin, let us not keep mourning
over it, let us not be occupied with ourselves,
but let us look to our victorious Lord, and
praise Him that He is still victorious. There is
one simple but all-inclusive guide, which the
word of God gives us to regulate our walk
with Jesus and to let us know when we have
sinned. Colossians 3:15 says, 'Let the peace of
Christ rule in your hearts.' Everything that
disturbs the peace of God in our hearts is sin,
no matter how small it is, and no matter how
little like sin it may at first appear to be. This
peace is to 'rule' our hearts, or (a more literal
translation), be the 'referee' in our hearts.
When the referee blows his whistle at a
football match the game has to stop, a foul has

been committed. When we lose our peace, God's referee in our hearts has blown his whistle! Let us stop immediately, ask God to show us what is wrong, confess to Him the sin He shows us, and then peace will be restored by the blood of Jesus, and we shall continue on our way with our cups running over. If, however, God does not give us His peace, it will be because we are not really broken.

Perhaps we have still to say 'sorry' to somebody else as well as to God. Or perhaps we still feel it is the other person's fault. But if we have lost our peace, it is obvious whose fault it is. We do not lose peace with God over another person's sin, but only over our own. God wants to show us our reactions, and only when we are willing to be cleansed of them will we have His peace. Oh, what a simple but searching thing it is to be ruled by the peace of God, by none other than the Holy Spirit Himself!

Former selfish ways, which we never bothered about, are now shown to us, and we cannot walk in them without the referee blowing his whistle. Grumbling, bossiness, carelessness, down to the smallest thing are all revealed as sins when we are prepared to let our days be ruled by the peace of God. Many times a day, and over the smallest things, we shall have to avail ourselves of the cleansing blood of Jesus, and we shall find ourselves walking the way of brokenness as never before. But Jesus will be manifested in all His loveliness and grace in that brokenness.

Many of us, however, have neglected the referee's whistle so often and for so long that we have ceased to hear it. Day after day we feel we have little need of cleansing and no reason to be broken. In that condition we are usually in a worse state than we ever imagine. It will need a great hunger for restored fellowship with God to possess our hearts before we will be willing to cry to God to show us where the blood of Jesus must be applied. He will show us, to begin with, just one thing, and it will be our obedience and brokenness on that one thing that will be the first step into revival for us.

Note

1. Some may be inclined to question whether it is right to call such things as self-consciousness, reserve, and fear, sins. 'Call them infirmities, disabilities, temperamental weaknesses, if you will,' some have said, 'but not sins. To do so would be to get us into bondage.' The reverse however is true. If these things are not sins, then we must put up with them for the rest of our lives, for there is no deliverance. But if these and other things like them are indeed sins, then we can be cleansed and delivered from them if we put them immediately 'under His precious blood' the moment we are conscious of them. And they *are* sins. Their source is unbelief and an inverted form of pride, and they have hindered and hidden Him countless times.

To Think About

As I have read this chapter, it seems clear that I am in one of three states:

1. I am filled with the Spirit and the peace of God is ruling in my heart.
2. I have temporarily grieved the Spirit and need to be restored through confession.
3. I have grieved the Spirit too often and done nothing about it, so I am no longer hearing God's convicting voice.

If I am in this third state, then I should pray that God would forgive me and restore my hunger for his peace and fellowship. Colossians 3:1 – 15 will be a great help if I read it slowly and apply all that it says.

Personal notes

_____

_____

_____

_____

_____

_____

_____

_____

3
THE WAY
OF FELLOWSHIP

When man fell and chose to make himself, rather than God, the centre of his life, the effect was not only to put man out of fellowship with God, but also out of fellowship with his fellow man. The story of man's first quarrel with God in Genesis chapter 3, is closely followed in the fourth chapter by the story of man's first quarrel with his fellow, when Cain murdered Abel. The Fall is simply that 'each of us has turned to his own way'.[1] If I want my own way rather than God's, it is quite obvious that I shall want my own way rather than someone else's. A person does not assert his independence of God only to surrender it to another, if he can help it. But a world in which each person wants his own way cannot be anything but full of tensions, barriers, suspicions, misunderstandings, clashes and conflicts.

Now the work of the Lord Jesus Christ on the Cross was not only to bring men back into

fellowship with God, but also into fellowship
with their fellow men. Indeed, it cannot do
one without the other. As the spokes get
nearer to the centre of a wheel, so they get
nearer to one another. So it is with us as we
get nearer to God. If we have not been
brought into vital fellowship with our fellow
Christians, it proves the extent to which we
have not been brought into vital fellowship
with God. The first epistle of John (what a
new light revival sheds on this scripture!)
insists on testing the depth and reality of a
person's fellowship with God by the depth and
reality of his fellowship with fellow believers.[2]
Some of us have come to see the close
connection between our relationship with our
fellow believers and our relationship with God.
Everything that comes as a barrier between us
and another, however small, comes as a barrier
between us and God. We have found that
where these barriers are not put right
immediately they get thicker and thicker until
we find ourselves shut off from God and
others by what seems to be a brick wall. Quite
obviously, if we allow new life to come to us, it
will have to be seen in a walk of oneness with
God and our brothers, with nothing
in-between.

Light and darkness

On what basis then can we have real fellowship
with God and our brother? Here 1 John 1:7
comes to us afresh. 'But if we walk in the

light, as He is in the light, we have fellowship
with one another, and the blood of Jesus, His
Son, purifies us from all sin.' What is meant
by light and darkness is that light reveals,
darkness hides. When anything reproves us,
shows us up as we really are — that is light.
'But everything exposed by the light becomes
visible'.[3] But whenever we do or say anything
(or do not say anything) to hide what we are
or what we've done — that is darkness.

Now the first effect of sin in our lives is
always to make us try to hide what we are. Sin
made our first parents hide behind the trees of
the garden, and it has had the same effect on
us ever since. Sin always involves us in being
unreal, pretending, duplicity, window-dressing,
excusing ourselves and blaming others — and
we can do that as much by our silence as by
our words or actions. This is what the
previous verse calls 'walking in darkness'.
With some of us, the sin in question may be
nothing more than self-consciousness
(anything with 'I' in it is sin) and the hiding,
nothing more than an assumed heartiness to
cover that self-consciousness, but it is walking
in darkness nonetheless.

In contrast to all this in us, verse five of this
chapter tells us that 'God is light', that is, God
is the all-revealing one who shows up every
man as he really is. It goes on to say, 'in Him
there is no darkness at all', that is, there is
absolutely nothing in God which can be at one
with the tiniest bit of darkness or concealment
in us.

Quite obviously, then, it is impossible for us to be walking in any degree of darkness and still have fellowship with God. While we are in that condition of darkness, we cannot have true fellowship with our brother either — for we are not real with him, and no-one can have fellowship with an unreal person. A wall of reserve separates him and us.

The only basis for fellowship

The only basis for real fellowship with God and man is to live out in the open with both. 'But if we walk in the light, as he is in the light, we have fellowship with one another.' To walk in the light is the opposite of walking in darkness. Spurgeon defines it in one of his sermons as 'the willingness to know and be known'. As far as God is concerned, this means that we are willing to know the whole truth about ourselves, and are open to conviction. We will submit to the first twinges of conscience. Everything He shows us to be sin we will deal with as sin — we will hide or excuse nothing. Such a walk in the light cannot do anything but discover sin increasingly in our lives, and we shall see things to be sin which we never thought to be so before. For that reason we might shrink from this walk, and be tempted to make for cover. But the verse goes on with the precious words, 'and the blood of Jesus, his Son, purifies us from all sin.' Everything that the light of God shows up as sin we can confess and carry to the fountain of blood, and it is gone, gone from God's sight and gone from our hearts. The power of this precious blood means that we can be purer than the driven snow. Thus, if we live continually in the light and allow ourselves to be cleansed by the blood, we can have fellowship with God.

The fellowship promised us here, however, is not only with God, but 'with one another', and that involves us in walking in the light with our fellow believers too. In any case we cannot be 'in the open' with God, and 'in the dark' with them. This means that we must be as willing to know the truth about ourselves from our brother as we are willing to know it from God. We must be prepared for him to hold the light to us (and we must be willing to do the same service for him) and challenge us in love about anything he sees in our lives which does not reflect that light. We must be willing not only to know, but also to be known by him for what we really are. That means we are not going to hide our inner selves from those with whom we ought to be in fellowship. We are not going to window dress and put on appearances. Nor are we going to white-wash and excuse ourselves. We are going to be honest about ourselves with others. We are willing to give up our spiritual privacy, pocket our pride, and risk our reputations for the sake of being open and transparent with our brothers and sisters in Christ. It means, too, that we are not going to cherish any wrong feeling in our hearts about another, but we are first going to claim deliverance from God and put it right with the one concerned. As we walk in this way, we shall find that we shall have fellowship with one another at an altogether new level, and we shall not love one another less, but infinitely more.

No bondage

Walking in the light is simply walking with Jesus. Therefore, there need be no bondage about it. We do not necessarily have to tell everybody everything about ourselves. The fundamental thing is our *attitude* of walking in the light, rather than the *act*. Are we willing to be in the open with our brother — and to speak out when God tells us to? That is the 'armour of light' — true transparency. This may sometimes be humbling, but it will help us to achieve a new reality with Christ, and a new self-knowledge. We have become so used to the fact that God knows all about us that it does not seem to register with us, and we inevitably end up by not knowing the truth about ourselves. But let a man begin to be absolutely honest about himself with just one other person, as God guides him, and he will come to a knowledge of himself and his sins that he never had before. He will begin to see more clearly than ever before where the redemption of Christ needs to be applied progressively to his life. This is the reason why James tells us to put ourselves under the discipline of 'confessing our sins to each other'.

In 1 John 1:7, of course, the purpose of 'walking in the light' is that we might 'have fellowship with one another'. And what fellowship it is when we walk this way together! Obviously, love will flow from one to another when each is prepared to be known as a sinner who repents at the Cross of Jesus. When the barriers are down and the masks are off, God has a chance to make us truly one in Him. But there is also the added joy of knowing that in such a fellowship we are 'safe'. We need have no fear that others may be thinking thoughts about us or having reactions towards us, which they are hiding from us. In a fellowship which is committed to walking in the light beneath the Cross, we know that if there is any thought about us, it will quickly be brought into the light, either in brokenness and confession (where there has been wrong or a lack of love), or else as a loving challenge, as something we ought to know about ourselves.

It must not, however, be forgotten that our walk in the light is first and foremost with the Lord Jesus. It is with Him first that we must get things settled, and it is His cleansing and victory that must first be obtained. Then when God guides us to open our hearts to others, we come to them with far more of a testimony than a confession (except where that is specifically necessary), and we praise God together.

Teams of two for revival

Jesus wants you to begin walking in the light with Him in a new way today. Join with one other — your Christian friend, the person you live with, your wife, your husband. Drop the mask. God has no doubt convicted you of one thing more than any other that you have to be honest with them about. Start there. Be a team of two to work for revival amongst your friends.

As others are broken at the Cross they will be added to your fellowship, as God leads. Get together from time to time for fellowship and to share your spiritual experience with real openness. In complete oneness pray together for others, and go out as a team with fresh testimony.

Through such a fellowship, God will begin to work wonderfully. As He saves and blesses others in this vital way, they can start to live and work as a fellowship too. As one billiard ball will move another, so one group will set off another group, until the whole of our land is covered with new life from the risen Lord Jesus.

Notes
1. Isaiah 53:6   2. 1 John 2:9, 3:14-15, 4:20
3. Ephesians 5:13

To Think About

My greatest enemy is my sinful self, what the Apostle Paul called the 'old self'. It makes excuses for my sin and blames others for everything that goes wrong in my life. If I listen to the insistent voice of the old self, then I will live a life which is displeasing to God, alienated from many others and full of misery. If I determine to put that old self to death, then I will have to join forces with the Holy Spirit and be ready to take responsibility for my own sin. Am I ready?

A prayer:

O Father, if I try to cover over and excuse my sin, will you uncover and expose it? When I begin to blame others, show me my faults. Wherever I am walking in darkness, will you shine your light? Help me daily to put to death my old self. Amen.

Personal notes

_____

_____

_____

_____

_____

_____

_____

4
THE HIGHWAY
OF HOLINESS

One of the things that we must learn if we are to live the victorious Christian life is its utter simplicity. How complicated we have made it! Great volumes are written; all sorts of technical phrases are used; we are told that the secret lies in this, or that, and so on. But to most of us, it is all so complicated that, although we know it in theory, we are unable to relate what we know to our practical daily living. In order to make the simple truths we have been considering even clearer we want to put them into picture form in this chapter.

The highway

An 'overall' picture of the life of victory, which is familiar to many of us, is that of the highway in Isaiah 35: 'And a highway will be there; it will be called the Way of Holiness'. The picture is that of a highway built up from the surrounding morass, the world. Though the highway is narrow and uphill, it is not beyond any of us to walk it, for 'whoever walks the road, although a fool, shall not go astray' (NKJV). Though there are many dangers if we get off the road, while we keep to the highway there is safety, for 'No lion will be there, nor will any ferocious beast get up on it'. Only one kind of person is barred from walking there, and that is the unclean one. 'The unclean will not journey on it'. This includes not only the sinner who does not know Christ as His saviour, but also the Christian who does, and yet is walking in unconfessed and uncleansed sin.

The only way on to the highway is up a small, dark, forbidding hill — the hill of Calvary. It is the sort of hill we have to climb on our hands and knees — especially our knees. If we are content with our present Christian life, if we do not desire with a desperate hunger to get on to the highway, we shall never get to our knees, and thus never climb the hill. But if we are dissatisfied, if we are hungry, then we will find ourselves climbing. Do not hurry. Let God make you really hungry for the highway. Let Him really drive you to your knees in longing prayer. Mere sightseers won't get very far. 'You will seek me and find me when you seek me with all your heart'.[1]

A low door

At the top of the hill, guarding the way to the highway, stands the Cross, gaunt and grim. There it stands, the divider of time and the divider of men. At the foot of the cross is a low door, so low that one has to stoop and crawl to get through it. It is the only entrance to the highway. We must go through it if we want to continue on our way. This door is called the 'door of the broken ones'. Only the broken can enter the highway. To be broken means 'not I, but Christ'.

There is in every one of us a proud, stiff-necked 'I'. The stiff neck began in the garden of Eden when Adam and Eve, who had always bowed their heads in surrender to God's will, stiffened their necks, struck out for independence and tried to be 'as gods'. All the way through the Bible God accuses His people of having the same stiff neck; and it reveals itself in us, too. We are hard and unyielding. We are sensitive and easily hurt. We get irritable, envious and critical. We are resentful and unforgiving. We strive in our own strength and attempt to do by our own efforts what should be left to God. We are self-indulgent — and how often that can lead to impurity!

Every one of these things, and many more, spring from this proud self within. If it were not there and Christ were in its place, we would not have these reactions. Before we can enter the highway, God must bend and break that stiff-necked self, so that Christ reigns instead. To be broken means to have no rights before God and man. It does not mean merely surrendering my rights to Him, but rather recognising that I haven't any, except to deserve hell. It means being nothing and having nothing that I call my own; neither time, money, possessions nor position.

In order to break our wills to His, God brings us to the foot of the Cross and there shows us what real brokenness is. We see those wounded hands and feet and that face of love crowned with thorns. We see the complete brokenness of the one who said 'Not my will, but yours be done',[2] as He drank the bitter cup of our sin to its dregs. So the way to be broken is to look on Him and to realise it was our sin which nailed Him there. Then as we see the love and brokenness of the God who died in our place, our hearts will be melted and we will want to be broken for Him, and we shall pray,

Oh, to be saved from myself, dear Lord,
Oh, to be lost in Thee,
Oh, that it might be no more I,
But Christ that lives in me.

Some of us have found that the prayer that He might break us is the one which God is most swift to answer.

A constant choice

Do not let us imagine, however, that we have to be broken only once as we go through the door. It will be a choice which is constantly before us. God brings His pressure to bear on us, but we have to make the choice. If someone hurts and slights us, we immediately have the choice of accepting the slight as a means of grace to humble us lower, or we can resist it and stiffen our necks again, with all the disturbance of spirit that that is bound to bring. Right the way through the day our brokenness will be tested, and it is no use pretending we are broken before God if we are not broken in our attitude to those around us. God nearly always tests us through other people. There are no second causes for the Christian. In the providence of God, His will is often made known to us through others with their many demands upon us. If you find yourself in a patch of unbrokenness, the only answer is to return to Calvary and see Christ broken for you. You will come away willing to be broken for Him.

Over the door of the broken ones is sprinkled the precious blood of the Lord Jesus. As we bend to crawl through, the blood cleanses us from all sin, for not only have we to bend to get through, but only the clean can walk on the highway. Maybe you have never known Jesus as your Saviour; maybe you have known Him for years; but in either case you are defiled by sin, the sins of pride, envy, resentment, impurity, etc. If you will give them all to Him who bore them on the Cross, He will whisper to you again what He once said on the Cross, 'It is finished', and your heart will be cleansed whiter than snow.

The gift of His fullness

So we reach the highway. There it stretches before us, a narrow, uphill road, bathed in

light, leading towards the heavenly Jerusalem.
The embankment on either side slopes away
into thick darkness. In fact, the darkness
creeps right to the very edges of the highway,
but on the highway itself all is light. Behind us
is the Cross, no longer dark and forbidding,
but radiant and glowing. We no longer see
Jesus stretched across its arms, but walking the
highway overflowing with resurrection life. In
His hands He carries a pitcher full of the water
of life. He comes right up to us and asks us to
hold out our hearts, and just as if we were
handing Him a cup, we present to Him our
empty hearts. He looks inside — which can be
a painful scrutiny — and where He sees we
have allowed His blood to cleanse our hearts,
He fills them with the water of life.

So we go on our way rejoicing and praising
God and overflowing with His new life. This
is revival, you and I full of the Holy Spirit all
the time, loving others and concerned for their
salvation. No struggling, no waiting; simply
giving Him each sin to cleanse in His precious
blood and accepting from His hands the free
gift of His fullness, then allowing Him to do
the work through us. As we walk along with
Him, He is always there continually filling our
cups so that they continually overflow.

So the rest of our Christian life now consists
simply of walking along the highway, with
hearts overflowing, bowing our necks to His
will all the time, constantly trusting the blood
to cleanse us, and living in complete oneness
with Jesus. There is nothing spectacular about

this life, no emotional experiences to crave and wait for. It is just plain day-to-day living the life the Lord intended us to live. This is real holiness.

Off the highway

But we may, and sometimes do, slip off the highway, for it is narrow. One little step aside and we are off the path and in darkness. It is always because of a failure in obedience somewhere or a failure to be weak enough to let God do everything. Satan is always beside the road, shouting at us, but he cannot touch us. But we can yield to his voice by an act of will. This is the beginning of sin and slipping away from Jesus.

Sometimes we find ourselves stiffening our necks towards another, sometimes to God Himself. Sometimes we are overwhelmed by jealousy or resentment. Sometimes we find ourselves tense and striving, without resting in Him. Immediately we are over the side, for nothing unclean can walk the highway. Our cup becomes dirty, ceases to overflow and we lose our peace with God. If we do not come back to the highway at once, we shall go further down the side. We must get back. How? The first thing to do is to ask God to show us what caused us to slip off; and He will, though it often takes Him time to make us see. Perhaps someone annoyed us, and we were irritated. God wants us to see that it was not the thing that the person did that matters, but our reaction to it. If we had been broken, we would not have been irritated. So, as we look longingly back to the highway, we see the Lord Jesus again, and we see what an ugly thing it is to get irritable, and that Jesus died to save us from being irritable. As we crawl up again to the highway on hands and knees, we come again to him and his blood for cleansing. Jesus is waiting there to fill our cup to overflowing again. Hallelujah!

Finding the highway again

No matter where we leave the highway, we will always find him calling us to come back and be broken again, and the blood will always be there to make us clean. This is the great secret of the highway — knowing what to do with sin, when sin has come in. The secret is always to take sin to the Cross, recognise its sinfulness, confess it to God, and count it gone, through the value of the blood of Jesus.

So, the real test all along the highway will be — are our cups running over? Is the peace of God ruling in our hearts? Have we love and concern for others? These things are the barometer of the highway. If they are disturbed, then sin has crept in somewhere — self-pity, self-seeking, self-indulgence in thought or deed, sensitiveness, touchiness, self-defence, striving in our own strength, self-consciousness, shyness, reserve, worry, fear and so on.

Our walk with others

An important thing about the highway which has not yet been mentioned is that we do not walk this highway alone. Others walk it with us. There is, of course, the Lord Jesus. But there are other people on this journey too, and the rule of the road is that fellowship with them is as important as fellowship with Jesus. Indeed, the two are intimately connected.

Our relationship with our fellows and our relationship with God are so linked that we cannot disturb one without disturbing the other. Everything that comes between ourselves and others, such as impatience, resentment or envy, comes between us and God. These barriers are sometimes no more than veils — veils through which we can still see to some extent. But if not removed immediately, they thicken into blankets and then into brick walls, and we are shut off from both God and our fellows, and shut in on ourselves. It is clear why these two relationships should be so linked, 'God is love', and the moment we fail to love others, we put ourselves out of fellowship with God — for God loves them, even if we do not.

But more than that, the effect of such sins is always to make us walk in darkness[3] — that is, to cover up and hide who we really are or what we are really feeling. That is the meaning of 'darkness' in Scripture, for, while the light reveals, the darkness hides. The first effect of sin in us is that we always hide, with the result that we pretend, wear masks and are not real with either God or man. And, of course, neither God nor man can have fellowship with an unreal person.

The way back into fellowship with the Lord Jesus will bring us again into fellowship with one another, too. All unlove must be recognised as sin and confessed as such that it may be covered by the blood of Jesus — and then it can be put right with others also. As we come back to the Lord Jesus like this, we shall find His love for others filling our hearts and wanting to express itself in our actions toward them, and we shall walk in fellowship together again.

So this is life on the highway. It is no new, astounding doctrine. It is not something new for us to preach. It is quite unspectacular. It is just a life to live day by day in whatever circumstances the Lord has put us. It does not contradict what we may have read or heard about the Christian life. It just puts into simple pictorial language the great truths of sanctification. To start to live this life now will mean revival in our lives. To continue to live it will be revival continued. Revival is simply you and I walking along the highway in complete oneness with the Lord Jesus and with one another, with cups continually cleansed and overflowing with the life and love of God.

Notes
1. Jeremiah 29:13   2. Luke 22:42   3. 1 John 2:9-11

To Think About

As I read Isaiah 35, I see that the highway of holiness is a wonderful path for my life. God promises that "gladness and joy will overtake" those who walk that way and that "sorrow and sighing will flee away". I want to walk that highway and I see that the entrance is just before me. All I have to do is bow my stiff neck and humble myself before God and others and I will climb that path to the highway.

A prayer:

O God, do not let my pride and self-righteousness prevent me from walking the Highway of Holiness. I choose to humble myself, please help me to stay on the path. Amen.

Personal notes

_____

_____

_____

_____

_____

_____

_____

_____

_____

5

THE DOVE AND
THE LAMB

Victorious living and effective evangelism are not the products of our better selves and hard work, but are simply the fruit of the Holy Spirit. We are not called upon to produce the fruit, but simply to bear it. It is God's fruit not ours. Nothing is more important, than that we should be continually filled with the Holy Spirit, or to keep to the metaphor, that the 'trees of the Lord are well watered' — by Him.[1]

How this may be true for us is graphically illustrated by the record, in John chapter one, of how the Holy Spirit came upon the Lord Jesus at His baptism. John the Baptist had seen Jesus coming to him and had said of Him, 'Look, the Lamb of God, who takes away the sin of the world'. Then, as he baptized Him, he saw the heavens opened and the Spirit of God descend like a dove and remain on Him.

The humility of God

What an evocative picture we have here — the
Dove descending and remaining upon the
Lamb! The lamb and the dove are surely the
gentlest of all God's creatures. The lamb
speaks of meekness and submissiveness, and
the dove speaks of peace (what more peaceful
sound than the cooing of a dove on a summer
day?). Does this not suggest that in the very
heart of God there is humility? When the
eternal God chose to reveal Himself in His
Son, He gave Him the name of the Lamb.

When it was necessary for the Holy Spirit to
come into the world He was revealed under the
emblem of the dove. Is it not obvious, then,
that the reason why we have to be humble in
order to walk with God is not merely because
God is so big and we are so small and that
humility befits such small creatures, but
because God, as seen in Jesus, is gentle and
humble in heart Himself.

The main lesson of this incident is that the
Holy Spirit, as the dove, could come upon
and remain upon the Lord Jesus only because
He was the Lamb. Had the Lord Jesus had
any other disposition than that of the lamb —
humility, submissiveness, and self-surrender —
the dove could never have remained on Him.
Being so gentle, the dove would have been
frightened away had not Jesus been gentle and
humble in heart.

This gives us a picture of how we need to be
in order for the same Holy Spirit to come

upon us and remain with us. The dove can remain with us only if we are willing to be like the lamb. How impossible that the Spirit should rest upon us while self remains unbroken!

The fruit of the unbroken self is the direct opposite of the gentleness of the dove. Read again in Galatians 5 the ninefold fruit of the Spirit (love, joy, peace, patience, kindness, goodness, faithfulness, gentleness and self-control) with which the dove longs to fill us! Then contrast it with the ugly works of the flesh (the New Testament name for the unbroken self) in the same chapter. It is the contrast of a snarling wolf with a gentle dove!

The disposition of the Lamb[2]

How clear it is, then, that the Holy Spirit will come upon us and remain upon us only as we are willing to be like the lamb every time He convicts us of sin! There is nothing so searching and humbling as to look at the Lamb on the way to Calvary for us, and to see in how many ways we have been unwilling to behave in the same way for Him.

Look at Him for a moment as the Lamb. He was the *simple Lamb*. A lamb is one of the simplest of God's creatures. It has no schemes or plans for helping itself — it exists in helplessness and simplicity. Jesus made Himself as nothing for us, and became the simple Lamb. He had no strength of His own or wisdom of His own, no schemes to get

Himself out of difficulties, just simple and continual dependence on the Father. 'The Son can do nothing by himself; he can do only what he sees his Father doing'.[3] But we — how complicated we are! What schemes have we had of helping ourselves and of getting ourselves out of difficulties! What efforts of our own we have resorted to, in order to live the Christian life and to do God's works, as if we were something and could do something! The dove had to take flight (at least as far as the conscious blessing of His presence was concerned) because we were not willing to be simple lambs.

Willing to be shorn

Then He was the *shorn Lamb*, willing to be shorn of His rights, His reputation, and every human liberty that was due to Him, just as a lamb is shorn of its wool. He never resisted. A lamb never does. When He was insulted for our sake He did not retaliate. When He suffered, He made no threats. He never said, 'You cannot treat me like that. Don't you know that I am the Son of God?' But on how many occasions have we been unwilling to be shorn of that which was ours by right. We were not willing for His sake to lose what was our own. We insisted, too, that we should be treated with the respect due to our position. We resisted, and we fought. The dove had to take flight from us, for we were not willing to

be shorn lambs, and we were left without
peace — hard and unloving.

He answered nothing

Then, He was the *silent lamb*. 'As a sheep
before her shearers is silent, so he did not open
his mouth'.[4] Facing the slander and lies of
men, we read, 'He made no reply'. He never
defended Himself, nor explained Himself. But
we have been anything but silent when others
have said unkind or untrue things about us.
Our voices have been loud in self-defence and
self-justification, and there has been anger in
our voices. We have made excuses when we
should have honestly admitted our wrong. On
every such occasion the dove had to take flight
and withdraw His peace and blessing from our
hearts, because we were not willing to be a
silent lamb.

No grudges

He was also the *spotless Lamb*. Not only did
nothing escape His lips, but there was nothing
in His heart except love for those who had
sent Him to the Cross. There was no
resentment towards them, no grudges, no
bitterness. Even as they were putting the nails
through his hands, He was murmuring, 'I
forgive you,' and he asked His Father to
forgive them too. He was willing to suffer
meekly for us. But how much resentment and
bitterness have we had in our hearts — toward

others, and over so much less than what they did to Jesus. Each reaction left a stain on our hearts, and the dove had to fly away because we were not willing to bear it and forgive it for Jesus' sake.

Return, O Dove!

These, then, are the acts and attitudes which drive the Holy Spirit from our lives, as far as present blessing is concerned, and they are all sin. Sin is the only thing that hinders the revival of His church. Our most important question is, 'How can the Dove return to our lives with His grace and power?' Again the answer is simply, 'the Lamb of God', for he is not only the simple Lamb, the shorn Lamb, the silent Lamb and the spotless Lamb, but above everything else He is the *substitute Lamb*.

To the Jew, the lamb that was offered to God was always a substitute lamb. Its meekness and submissiveness were only incidental to its main purpose, that of being slain for sin and of having its blood sprinkled on the altar to atone for it. The humility of the Lord Jesus in becoming our lamb was necessary because only on the Cross might He become our substitute, our scapegoat, carrying our sins in His own body on the tree, so that there might be forgiveness for our sins and cleansing from all their stains, when we repent. God wants, moreover, to take us back to the Cross and show us our sins wounding and hurting the Lamb. 'Were you there when they crucified my Lord?' asks the song. The answer is 'Yes, we were.' By our unwillingness to 'break', we show that we were part of that crowd killing Him at Calvary. And our gentle Lamb was willing for them, and us to do it, in order that, when at last we repent, there might be precious blood to secure our forgiveness and to cleanse us from all sin. May this solemn thought break our proud hearts in repentance! For it is only when we have seen these sins of ours in the heart of Jesus, so that we are broken and willing to repent of them and put them right, that the blood of the Lamb cleanses us from them and the Dove returns with peace and blessing to our hearts.

He humbled Himself to the manger,
And even to Calvary's tree;
But I am so proud and unwilling,
His humble disciple to be.

He yielded His will to the Father,
And chose to abide in the Light;
But I prefer wrestling to resting,
And try by myself to do right.

Lord break me, then cleanse me and fill me
and keep me abiding in Thee;
That fellowship may be unbroken,
and Thy Name be hallowed in me.

A saintly African Christian once told a congregation that as he was climbing the hill

to the meeting he heard steps behind him. He
turned and saw a man carrying a very heavy
load up the hill on his back. He was full of
sympathy for him and spoke to him. Then he
noticed that His hands were scarred, and he
realised that it was Jesus. He said to Him,
'Lord, are you carrying the world's sin up the
hill?' 'No,' said the Lord Jesus, 'not the *world's*
sin, just yours!' As that African simply told
the vision that God had just given him, the
people's hearts and his heart were broken as
they saw their sins at the Cross.

Our hearts need to be broken too, and only
when they are, shall we be willing for the
confessions, the apologies, the reconciliations,
and the restitutions that are involved in true
repentance of sin. Then, when we have been
willing to humble ourselves, as the Lord
humbled Himself, the Dove will return to us.

> Return, O heavenly Dove, return,
> Sweet messenger of rest!
> I hate the sins that made Thee mourn,
> And drove Thee from my breast.

Ruled by the Dove

One last word. The dove is the emblem of
peace, which suggests that if the blood of Jesus
has cleansed us and we are walking with the
Lamb in humility, the sign of the Spirit's
presence and fullness will be peace. This is
indeed to be the test of our walk all the way.
'Let the peace of Christ rule [or arbitrate] in

your hearts."[5] If the Dove ceases to sing in our hearts at any time, if our peace is broken, then it can be only because of sin. In some way we must have departed from the humility of the Lamb, and we must ask God to show us in what way. When we repent and bring that sin to the Cross the Dove will return to His rightful place in our hearts and once more we shall have peace with God. In this way we shall know that continuous abiding of the Spirit's presence, which is open even to fallen men through the immediate and constant application of the precious blood of Jesus.

From today, shall we not begin to allow our lives to be ruled by the heavenly Dove, the peace of God, and allow Him to be the judge all day long? If we do, we shall find ourselves to be walking in a path of constant conviction and much humbling. However, in this way we shall come into real conformity with the Lamb of God, and we shall know the only victory that is worth anything — the conquest of self.

Notes

1. Psalm 104:16   2. The headings in this section relating to the characteristics of the Lamb I owe to an address given by my friend Marshall Shallis of England.   3. John 5:19
4. Isaiah 53:7   5. Colossians 3:15

To Think About

In Galatians 5, the fruit of my sinful nature is listed: "sexual immorality, impurity and debauchery; idolatry and witchcraft; hatred, discord, jealousy, fits of rage, selfish ambition, dissensions, factions and envy; drunkenness, orgies and the like."

But if I live with the peace of God ruling in my heart then I will bear the fruit of the Spirit which is: "love, joy, peace, patience, kindness, goodness, faithfulness, gentleness and self control."

Which list most describes me, not only in the way I act or appear when with others, but in my most private thoughts?

Thank God that Jesus is the substitute lamb! Whenever any of the fruits of the sinful nature creep into my life, God is willing and able to forgive me through the sacrifice of Jesus.

Personal notes

_____

_____

_____

_____

_____

_____

_____

6
REVIVAL IN THE HOME

Thousands of years ago, in the most beautiful garden the world has ever known, lived a man and a woman. Formed in the likeness of their creator, they lived solely to reveal Him to His creation and to each other, and thus to glorify Him every moment of the day. Humbly they accepted their position — one of complete submission and yielding to His will. Because they always submitted their wills to His, because they lived for Him and not for themselves, they were also completely submitted to each other. Thus in that first home in that beautiful garden there was absolute harmony, peace, love and oneness, not only with God but also with each other.

Then one day the harmony was shattered, for the serpent stole into that God-centred home, and with him came sin. And now, because they had lost their peace and fellowship with God, they lost it with each other. They no longer lived for God and no

longer even for each other — they only lived
for themselves. They each became their own
gods. Instead of peace, harmony, love and
oneness, there was now discord and hate — in
other words, SIN!

Revival begins at home

It was into the home that sin first came. It is
in the home that we sin more than perhaps
anywhere else, and it is to the home that
revival first needs to come. Revival is
desperately needed in the church, in the
country and in the world, but a revived church
with unrevived homes would be sheer
hypocrisy. It is the hardest place and the most
costly, but also the most necessary place to
begin.

Before we go on, let us remind ourselves
again of what revival really is. It simply means
new life in hearts where the spiritual life has
ebbed — but not a new life of self-effort or
self-initiated activity. It is not man's life, but
God's life, the life of Jesus filling us and
flowing through us. That life shows itself in
fellowship and oneness with those with whom
we live — nothing between us and God, and
nothing between us and others. The home is
the place before all others where revival
should be experienced.

How different is the experience of so many
of us professing Christians in our homes —
little irritations, frayed tempers, selfishness and
resentments exist. Even where there is nothing

definitely wrong between us, there is simply
not that complete oneness and fellowship that
ought to characterise Christians living
together. All the things that come between us
and others, come between us and God, and
spoil our fellowship with Him, so that our
hearts are not overflowing with the divine life.

What is wrong with our homes?

Now when it comes down to it, what is wrong
with our homes? When we talk about homes
we mean the relationship which exists between
a husband and wife, a parent and child, a
brother and sister, or between any others who,
through various circumstances, are compelled
to live together.

The first thing that is wrong with so many
families is that they are not really open with
one another. We live so largely behind drawn
blinds. The others do not know us for what
we are, and we do not intend that they should.
Even those living in the most intimate
relationships with us do not know what goes
on inside — our difficulties, battles, failures,
nor what the Lord Jesus has to cleanse us from
so frequently. This lack of transparency and
openness is, as always, the result of sin. The
first effect of the first sin was that Adam and
Eve hid from God behind the trees of the
garden. They who had been so transparent
with God and with each other were then
hiding from God because of sin. If they hid
from God you can be sure that they soon

began to hide from each other. There were
reactions and thoughts in Adam's heart that
Eve was never allowed to know, and there were
similar things hidden in Eve's heart too. So it
has been ever since. Having something to hide
from God, we also hide it from one another.
Behind that wall of reserve, which acts like a
mask, we cover our real selves. Sometimes we
hide in the most extraordinary way behind a
façade of humour. We are afraid to be serious
because we do not want others to get too close
and see us as we really are, and so we keep up
a game of pretence. We are not real with one
another, and no-one can have fellowship with
an unreal person, and so oneness and close
fellowship are impossible in the home. This is
what the Scripture calls 'walking in darkness'
— for the darkness is anything which hides.

The failure to love

The second thing that is wrong with our
homes is our failure really to love one another.
'Well,' you might say, 'that could never be said
of our home, for no-one could love anyone
more than my husband and I love each other!'
But wait a minute! It depends on what you
mean by love. Love is not just a sentimental
feeling, nor even a strong passion. The
famous passage in 1 Corinthians 13 tells us
what real love is, and if we test ourselves by its
standard we may find that, after all, we are
hardly loving one another at all, and our
behaviour is totally the opposite — and the

opposite of love is hate! Let us look at some of the things that this passage tells us about love.

'Love is patient,
love is kind.
It does not envy,
it does not boast,
it is not proud.
It is not rude,
it is not self-seeking,
it is not easily angered,
it keeps no record of wrongs.'

How do we stand up to these tests in our homes? So often we act in the very opposite way.

We are often impatient with one another and even unkind in the way we answer back or react.

How much jealousy, too, there can be in a home. A husband and wife can be jealous of each other's gifts, even of their spiritual progress. Parents may be jealous of their children, and how often there is bitter jealousy between brothers and sisters.

Also, 'love is not rude', behaving with courtesy, what about that? Courtesy is just love in little things, but it is in the little things that we trip up. We think we can 'let up' at home.

How proud we so often are! Pride comes out in all sorts of ways. We think we know best. We want our way, and we nag or boss others, and nagging or bossing leads on to the tendency to despise them. Our very attitude of superiority sets us above them. Then, when at the bottom of our hearts we despise someone, we blame them for everything — and yet we think we love.

Then what about not being selfish? Many times a day we put our wishes and interests before those of others.

How 'easily angered' we are! How quick to be irritated by something in another! How often we allow the unkind thought, the resentful feeling over something the other has done, or left undone! Yet we profess that there are no failures of love in our homes. These things happen every day and we think nothing of them. They are all of them the opposite of love, and the opposite of love is hate.

Impatience is hate. Envy is hate. Conceit and self-will are hate, and so are selfishness, irritability, and resentment! And hate is SIN. 'Anyone who claims to be in the light but hates his brother is still in the darkness.'[1]

What tensions, barriers and discord result, and fellowship with God and others is made impossible.

The only way out

Now the question is, 'Do we want new life and revival, in our homes?' We must examine our hearts. Are we prepared to continue in this state, or are we really hungry for new life, His life, in our homes? Unless we are really

hungry, we will not be willing to take the
necessary steps. The first step is to call sin, sin
(our own sin, not the other person's) and go
with it to the Cross, and trust the Lord Jesus
to cleanse us from it there and then.

As we bow our heads at the Cross, His
selfless love for others, His patience and
forbearance flow into our hearts. His precious
blood cleanses us from our unloving attitude
and ill will, and the Holy Spirit fills us with the
very nature of Jesus. 1 Corinthians 13 is
nothing less than the nature of Jesus, and it is
a gift for us, for His nature *is* ours, if He is
ours. We can receive this gift every single time
sin and lack of love begin to creep in, for this
cleansing fountain of blood is available to us
all the time.

All this will commit us very definitely to
walking the way of the Cross in our homes.
Again and again we will see places where we
must give up our rights, as Jesus gave up His
for us. We shall have to see that the thing in us
that reacts so sharply to another's selfishness
and pride is simply our own selfishness and
pride, which we are unwilling to sacrifice. We
shall have to accept another's ways and actions
as God's will for us and meekly submit to it.
This does not mean that we must accept other
people's selfishness as God's will for *them* —
far from it — but only as God's will for *us*. As
far as others are concerned, God will probably
want to use us, if we are broken, to help them
see their need. Certainly if we are a parent we
shall often need to correct our child with

firmness. But none of this should be from selfish motives, but only out of love for others and a longing for their good. Our own convenience and rights must be yielded continuously. Only in this way will the love of the Lord Jesus be able to fill us and be expressed through us.

When we have been broken at Calvary we must be willing to put things right with others — sometimes even with our own children. This is so often the test of our brokenness. Brokenness is the opposite of hardness. Hardness says, 'It's your fault!' Brokenness, however, says, 'It's my fault!' What a different atmosphere will begin to reign in our homes when they hear us admit, 'It's my fault!' Let us remember that at the Cross there is only room for one at a time. We cannot say, 'I was wrong, but you were wrong too. You must come as well!' No, we must go alone, saying, 'I'm wrong.' God will work in others more through our brokenness than through anything else we can do or say. We may, however, have to wait — perhaps for a long time. But that should only cause us to understand more perfectly how God feels, for, as someone has said, 'He, too, has had to wait for a long time since His great attempt to put things right with man two thousand years ago, although there was no wrong on His side'. But God will surely answer our prayer and bring the other person to Calvary too. There we shall be one; there the barrier between us will be broken down; there we shall be able to walk in the light, in true transparency with Jesus and with one another, loving each other deeply from the heart. Sin is almost the only thing we have in common with everyone else and so the only place where we can be one, is at the feet of Jesus, where sin is cleansed.

Note
1. 1 John 2:9

To Think About

In 1 Corinthians 13, love is described as God intends it to be and as Jesus demonstrated it. Does it describe my relationships at home? Am I patient, kind, not rude, not self-seeking? When I am at home and with those who know me best, my real inner self is most likely to be expressed. If I am beginning to experience revival, it will be felt most at home.

Do I want revival badly enough to humble myself before my family? Am I willing to ask forgiveness if I am impatient, or rude or selfish? Am I willing to ask members of my family to hold me accountable to God's high standards of love?

Personal notes

_____

_____

_____

_____

_____

A prayer:
My Father, the life of brokenness and humility is probably most difficult to embrace at home. I do not find it easy to be humble and loving at all times with my family. Help me to embrace your path for me, especially with my family. Amen.

7
THE SPECK
AND THE PLANK

There is something in our friend's eye!
Though it is only something tiny — what
Jesus called a speck — how painful it is,
and how helpless they are until it is removed!
It is surely our responsibility as a friend to do
all we can to remove it. How grateful they are
when we have succeeded. We would be equally
grateful if they did the same service for us.

In the light of that, it seems clear that the
real point of the well-known passage in
Matthew 7:3-5 about the plank and the speck
is not to forbid us from trying to remove the
fault in the other person, but rather the
opposite; that at all costs we should do this
service for one another. True, its first emphasis
seems to be a condemnation of
judgementalism, but when that has been dealt
with, the passage ends by saying, 'then you will
see clearly to remove the speck from your
brother's eye'. According to the New
Testament, we are meant to care so much for

others, that we are willing to do all that we can to remove from their eyes the speck which is marring their vision and hindering their blessing. We are told to 'admonish one another' and 'encourage one another', 'wash one another's feet' and 'to spur one another on towards love and good deeds'. The love of Jesus poured out in our hearts will make us want to help each other in this way.

What a blessing we could bring to others if we were willing to challenge one another in humility as God leads. A humble Swiss man named Nicholas of Basle, one of the Society of the Friends of God, crossed the mountains to Strasburg and entered the church of Dr Tauler, the popular preacher of that city. He challenged Dr Tauler. 'Before you can do your greatest work for God, the world, and this city, you must die — die to yourself, your gifts, your popularity, and even to your own goodness. When you have learned the full meaning of the Cross, you will have a new power with God and man.' That humble challenge from an obscure Christian changed Dr Tauler's life. He did indeed learn to die and as a result was greatly instrumental in preparing the way for Luther and the Reformation. In this passage from Matthew, the Lord Jesus tells us how we may help one another in this way.

What is the plank?

First, however, the Lord Jesus tells us that it is only too possible to try to take a tiny speck of sawdust out of the other's eye when there is a plank, a great length of timber in our own. When that is the case, we haven't a chance of removing the speck from the other, because we cannot see straight ourselves, and in any case it is sheer hypocrisy to attempt to do so.

Now we all know what Jesus meant by the speck in the other person's eye. It is some fault we suppose that we can discern. It may be an act committed against us, or some attitude adopted towards us. But what did the Lord Jesus mean by the plank in our eye? I suggest that the plank in our eye is simply our unloving reaction to the other person's speck.

Without doubt there is a wrong in the other person, but our reaction to that wrong is wrong too! The speck in them has provoked in us resentment, or coldness, or criticism, or bitterness, or evil speaking, or ill will — which are all variants of the basic ill, a failure to love. And that, says the Lord Jesus, is far, far worse than the tiny wrong (sometimes quite unconscious) that provoked it. In the Greek a speck means a little splinter, whereas a plank means a rafter. By this comparison the Lord Jesus means to tell us that our unloving reaction to the other's wrong is what a great rafter is to a little splinter! Every time we point one of our fingers at another and say, 'It's your fault', three of our fingers are pointing back at us. God have mercy on us for the many times when we have been guilty of this and in our hypocrisy have tried to deal with the other person's fault, when God saw there was something far worse in our own hearts.

But let us not think that a plank is of necessity some *violent* reaction on our part. A plank can be the first hint of a resentment or the first flicker of an unkind thought, or the first suggestion of unloving criticism. Where this is so, it only distorts our vision, and we shall never see others as they really are, deeply loved by God. If we speak to them with sin in our hearts, it will only provoke them to adopt the same hard attitude to us, for it is a law of human relationships that 'with the measure you use [to judge others] it will be measured to you'.

Take it to Calvary

'First take the plank out of your own eye'. That must be where we begin. We must recognise our unloving reaction to others as sin. On our knees we must take it to Calvary, see Jesus there, and get a glimpse of what that sin cost Him. At His feet we must repent and be broken afresh. We must trust the Lord Jesus to cleanse it away in His precious blood and fill us with love for that person. And He will, and does, if we will claim His promise. Then we shall probably need to go to the other person in an attitude of repentance, confess the sin that has been in our heart and what the blood has accomplished, and ask for their forgiveness as well. Very often people around us, and sometimes even our own hearts, will tell us that the sin we are confessing is not nearly so bad as the other's wrong — which is still to be confessed. But we have been to Calvary, indeed we are learning to live under the shadow of Calvary, and we have seen our sin there and we can no longer compare our sin with another's.

As we take these simple steps of repentance, *then* we can see clearly to cast the speck out of the other's eye, for the plank in our eye has gone. In that moment God will shed new light on the other's need. Then we may see that the speck we were so conscious of before is virtually non-existent — it was merely the projection of something that was in us. Or, we may have revealed to us hidden and underlying things of which the other person was hardly aware. Then, as God leads us, we must lovingly and humbly challenge them, so that these things might be revealed to them too. They can then bring them to that fountain for sin, the Cross, and find deliverance. At this point they will be more willing than ever to accept our challenge — indeed, if they are humble, they will be grateful to us, for they will know now that there is no selfish motive in our heart, but only love and concern for them.

When God is leading us to challenge someone, we must not allow fear to hold us back. Let us not argue or press our point. Let us just say what God has told us to and leave it at that. It is God's work, not ours, to cause others to see. It takes time to be willing to bend 'the proud, stiff-necked I'. When we in turn are challenged, let us not be defensive or try to explain ourselves. Let us accept it in silence, thanking the other, then take it to God and ask Him about it. If they were right, let us be humble enough to go and tell them, and then praise God together. There is no doubt that we need each other desperately. There are blind spots in all our lives that we shall never see, unless we are prepared for God to challenge us through others.

To Think About

*How long has it been since I was lovingly
rebuked by a fellow Christian? And when was
the last time I took another person's faults to
God in prayer? Did I deal with my own
unhelpful reactions to that fault and then go to
my brother or sister with a desire to help
them?*

As rare as such openness is, it is nevertheless the
way God's Word teaches us to relate to one another.

A prayer:

*O Father, help me always to be aware of planks in
my own eye, and enable me to remove them. But
also help me to overcome my fear of approaching
others with a desire to help them overcome their
faults. Grant me wisdom and love that I might
always respond well to rebuke from another, and
that I might be ready to admonish others in your
time and your way. Amen.*

Personal notes

_____

_____

_____

_____

_____

_____

8

ARE YOU WILLING TO BE A SERVANT?

Nothing is more clear in the New Testament than the fact that the Lord Jesus expects us to take the humble position of servants. This is not just an extra obligation which we may take or leave as we please. It is the very heart of that new relationship which the disciple is to take up with respect to God and to his fellows, if he is to know fellowship with Christ and any degree of holiness in his life. When we understand the humbling and self-emptying that is involved in being a true servant, it becomes evident that only those who are prepared to live quite definitely under the shadow of Calvary, contemplating the humility and brokenness of the Lord Jesus, will be willing to accept such a position.

As we approach this subject and its personal application in detail to our lives, there are three preliminary things which need to be said to prepare us to understand the low and humbling position which He wants us to take.

In the Old Testament two sorts of servants are mentioned. There are the *hired servants*, who have wages paid to them and have certain rights. Then there are the *bond-servants*, or slaves, who have no rights, who receive no wages, and have no right of appeal. The Hebrews were forbidden to make bond-servants of their own race. They were only permitted to take such slaves from the Gentiles. When, however, we come to the New Testament, the word in Greek for servant of the Lord Jesus Christ is not 'hired servant' but 'bond-servant'. This means that our position is one where we have no rights and no chance to appeal, where we are the absolute property of our Master, to be treated and disposed of just as He wishes.

Further, we shall see even more clearly what our position is to be, when we understand that we are to be the bond-servants of one who was Himself willing to be a bond-servant. The following Scriptures reveal the amazing humility of the Lord Jesus 'who being in very nature God, did not consider equality with God something to be grasped, but made himself nothing, taking the very nature of a servant . . . .'[1]

He was without rights, willing to be treated as the will of the Father and the malice of men might decree, for the purpose of serving men and bringing them back to God. And you and I are to be the bond-servants of Him who remains a bond-servant, whose disposition is always that of humility and whose activity is the humbling of Himself to serve the ones He created. How very low, then, is our true position! How this shows us what it means to be ruled by the Lord Jesus!

This leads us on to something further. Our servanthood to the Lord Jesus is to express itself in our servanthood to our fellows. Paul says, 'For we do not preach ourselves, but Jesus Christ as Lord, and ourselves as your servants for Jesus' sake'.[2] The humility we adopt in relation to the Lord, is judged by the humility we display in our relationship with others. If we are unwilling to serve others in costly and humbling ways, He considers us to be unwilling to serve Him. In this way we put ourselves out of fellowship with Him.

We are now in a position to apply all this more personally to our lives. God spoke to me some time ago through Luke 17:7-10.

'Suppose one of you had a servant ploughing or looking after the sheep. Would he say to the servant when he comes in from the field, "Come along now and sit down to eat"? Would he not rather say, "Prepare my supper, get yourself ready and wait on me while I eat and drink; after that you may eat and drink"? Would he thank the servant because he did what he was told to do? So you also, when you have done everything you were told to do should say, "We are unworthy servants; we have only done our duty."'

I see here five marks of the bond-servant. *First of all, he must be willing to have one thing on top of another put on him, without being given any consideration.* On top of a hard day in the field the servant in the parable had immediately to prepare his master's meal, and even then serve it to him — all before he was allowed any food himself. He just went and did it, expecting nothing else. How unwilling we are for this to happen to us! How quickly there are murmurings and bitterness in our hearts when that sort of thing is expected of us. But the moment we start murmuring, we are acting as though we had rights, and a bond-servant hasn't any!

Secondly, in doing this he must be willing not to be thanked for it. How many times we serve others with self-pity in our hearts, and then complain bitterly when they take it for granted, and do not thank us for it. But a bond-servant must be willing to accept that. Hired servants may expect something, but not bond-servants.

And, thirdly, having done all this, he must not accuse the other of selfishness. As I read the passage, I could not help feeling that the master was rather selfish and inconsiderate, but there is no such accusation from the bond-servant. He exists to serve the interests of his master, and the selfishness or otherwise of his master is not his concern. But what about us? We can perhaps allow ourselves to be 'put upon' by others, and are even willing not to be thanked for what we do, yet how we accuse the other in our minds of selfishness! But that is not the place of the bond-servant who is to find in the selfishness of others further opportunity to identify with His Lord as the servant of all.

There is, however, a fourth step which we must take ourselves. There is no ground for pride or self-congratulation, *but we must confess that we are unworthy servants,* that is that we are of no real use to God or man in ourselves. We must confess again and again that 'nothing good lives in me, that is, in my sinful nature.'[3] If we have acted as bond–servants, it is not due to us, whose hearts are naturally proud and stubborn, but only to the Lord Jesus, who dwells in us and who has made us willing.

The knock-out blow to self is dealt by the fifth and final step. *We must admit that in acting and enduring with meekness and humility, we have not done one iota more than it was our duty to do.* God made man in the first place simply that he might be His bond-servant.

Man's sin has simply consisted of his refusal to be God's bond-servant. Therefore his restoration can only be a restoration to the position of a bond-servant. Man has not done anything particularly praiseworthy when he agrees to accept such a position, for he was created and redeemed for that very place.

This is the way of the Cross. It is the way that God's lowly bond-servant first trod for us, and should not we, the bond-servants of that bond-servant, tread it still? Does it seem hard

and forbidding, this way down? Be assured, it
is the only way up. It was the way by which
the Lord Jesus reached the throne, and it is the
way by which we, too, reach the place of
spiritual power, authority and fruitfulness.
Those who tread this path are radiant, happy
souls, overflowing with the life of their Lord.
They have found that 'he who humbles himself
shall be exalted' is as true for them as for their
Lord. Humility and repentance must become
a way of life.

We shall not enter into more abundant life
merely by resolving to be more humble in the
future. We must first repent of past attitudes
and actions which still persist, if only by our
unwillingness to apologise for them. The Lord
Jesus did not take the very nature of a servant
merely to give us an example, but so that He
might die for these very sins upon the cross,
and open a fountain of His precious blood
where they can all be washed away. But that
blood cannot be applied to the sins of our
proud hearts until we have been broken in
repentance over what has already happened
and over what we already are. This will mean
allowing the light of God to go through every
part of our hearts and into every part of our
relationships.

It will mean that we shall have to see that
the sins of pride, which God will show us,
made it necessary for Jesus to come from
heaven and die on the Cross that they might be
forgiven. It will mean not only asking Him to
forgive us but asking others too. That will be

humbling indeed. But as we crawl through the 'door of the broken ones', we shall emerge into the light and glory of the highway of holiness and humility.

Notes
1. Philippians 2:6-7   2. 2 Corinthians 4:5   3. Romans 7:18

To Think About

It is clearly God's will that I should become his bond-servant. If I am willing, then he is committed to help me. If I ask, then he is willing to shine his light into my heart and show me those attitudes, words and actions which are not servant-like. Therefore, I want to pray:

My Father in heaven, I know I have not lived as a bond-servant. I have not done all that you have commanded and I have often refused to serve others, especially when they seemed demanding or ungrateful. Please forgive me and help me to be a bond-servant; show me every unservant-like attitude. Help me to be more like Jesus, my master, today. Amen.

Personal notes

_____

_____

_____

_____

_____

_____

_____

_____

_____

9

THE POWER OF THE BLOOD OF THE LAMB

The message and challenge of revival which faces many of us in these days is searching in its perfect simplicity. It is this, that there is only one thing in the world that can hinder the Christian from walking in victorious fellowship with God, and being filled with the Holy Spirit — and that is sin in whatever form. There is only one thing in the world that can cleanse the Christian from sin, and so bring liberty and victory — and that is the power of the blood of the Lord Jesus. It is, however, most important for us that we should see what gives the blood of Christ its mighty power with God on behalf of men, for only then shall we understand the conditions through which its full power may be experienced in our lives.

How many achievements and how many blessings the Scripture attributes to the power of the blood of the Lord Jesus! By the power of His blood peace is made between man and God.[1] By its power there is forgiveness of sins

and eternal life for all who put their faith in
the Lord Jesus.[2] By the power of His blood
Satan is overcome.[3] By its power there is
continual cleansing from all sin for us.[4] By the
power of His blood we may be set free from
the tyranny of an evil conscience in order to
serve the living God.[5] By its infinite power
with God the most unworthy have confidence
to enter the Most Holy place of God's
presence and live there all day long.[6]

What gives the blood its power? How may
we experience this power to the full in our
lives? Too often that precious blood does not
have its sin-cleansing, peace-giving,
life-imparting power in our hearts, and too
often we do not find ourselves in God's
presence and fellowship all day long.

The power's source

The answer to the first question is suggested
by the phrase in the book of Revelation which
describes the blood of Christ by the tender
expression, 'the blood of the Lamb'.[7] Not the
blood of the warrior, but the blood of *the
Lamb*! In other words that which gives the
precious blood its power with God for men is
the lamb-like disposition of the one who shed
it. The title 'the Lamb', so frequently given to
the Lord Jesus in Scripture, is first of all
descriptive of His work — that of being a
sacrifice for our sin. When an Israelite who
had sinned wanted to get right with God, it
was the blood of a lamb (sometimes that of a

goat) which had to be shed and sprinkled on the altar. Jesus is the divine fulfilment of all those lambs that men offered — the Lamb of God, who takes away the sin of the world.[8] But the title 'the Lamb' has a deeper meaning. It describes His character. He is the Lamb in that He is gentle and humble in heart,[9] meek and unresisting, and all the time surrendering His own will to the Father's will, for the blessing and saving of men[10]. Anyone but the Lamb would have resented and resisted the treatment men gave Him, but He, in obedience to the Father,[11] and out of love for us, did neither. Men did what they liked to Him, and for our sakes He yielded continually. When He was insulted, He did not retaliate. When He suffered, He made no threats. No standing up for His rights, no hitting back, no resentment, no complaining! How different from us! When the Father's will and the malice of men pointed to dark Calvary, the Lamb meekly bowed his head, willing for that too. It was as the Lamb that Isaiah saw Him, when he prophesied, 'He was led like a lamb to the slaughter, and as a sheep before her shearers is silent, so he did not open his mouth.'[12] The scourging, the scoffing, the spitting, the hair plucked from His cheeks, the weary last march up the hill, the nailing and the lifting up, the piercing of His side and the flowing of His blood! None of these things would ever have happened, had He not been the Lamb. And all that to pay the price of *my* sin! So we see that He is not merely the Lamb because He died on the Cross, but he died upon the Cross because He is the Lamb.

Let every mention of the blood call to mind the deep humility and self-surrender of the Lamb, for it is this nature and disposition that gives the blood its wonderful power with God for men. Hebrews 9:14 for ever links the blood of Christ with His self-offering to God, 'How much more, then, will the blood of Christ, who through the eternal Spirit *offered himself* unblemished to God cleanse our consciences from acts that lead to death, so that we may serve the living God?' Humility, lamb-likeness, the surrender of our wills to God are what He looks for supremely from us. It was to manifest all this that God created the first man. It was his refusal to walk this path that constituted his first sin, and it has been the heart of sin ever since. It was to restore this disposition on earth that Jesus came. It was simply because the Father saw this in Him that He could say, 'This is my Son, whom I love; with him I am well pleased.'[13] It was because the shedding of His blood so supremely expressed this disposition that it is so utterly precious to God and so effective for man and his sin.

The second question

We come now to the second question — how can we experience its full power in our lives? Our hearts surely tell us the answer, as we look at the Lamb, bowing His head for us at

Calvary — only by being willing to have the same disposition that ruled Him and by bowing our heads in brokenness just as He bowed His. Just as it is the disposition of the Lamb which gives the blood its power, so it is only as we are willing to share in the same disposition that we shall know its full power in our lives. And we *can* participate in the divine nature,[14] for it has been made transferable to us by His death. Consider the fruits of the Holy Spirit, mentioned in Galatians 5 — love, joy, peace, patience, kindness, goodness, faithfulness, gentleness and self-control. What are these other than the expressions of the lamb-like nature of the Lord Jesus, with which the Holy Spirit wants to fill us? Let us never forget that the Lord Jesus, though exalted to the throne of God, is still the Lamb (the book of Revelation tells us that) and He wants to see us changed into His likeness.

Are we willing?

But are we willing for this to happen? There is a hard, unyielding self, which stands up for itself and resists others, that will have to be broken, if we are to be willing to accept the disposition of the Lamb, and if the precious blood is to reach us in cleansing power. We may pray at length to be cleansed from some sin and for peace to be restored to our hearts, but unless we are willing to be broken on the point in question, and then be made partakers of the Lamb's humility, nothing will happen.

Every sin we ever commit is the result of the
hard, unbroken self taking up some attitude of
pride. We shall not find peace through the
blood until we are willing to see the source of
each sin, and reverse the wrong attitude that
caused it by a specific repentance, which will
always be humbling. We only have to walk in
the light, and be willing for God to reveal any
sin that may be in our lives, and we shall find
ourselves asked by the Lord to perform all
sorts of costly acts of repentance and
surrender, often over what we term small and
trivial matters. Their importance, however,
can be gauged by what it costs our pride to
put them right.

He may show us a confession or apology
that has to be made to someone, or an act of
restitution that has to be done.[15] He may show
us that we must climb down over something
and yield up our supposed rights to it (Jesus
had no rights — why should we have any?).
He may show us that we must go to the one
who has done wrong and confess to him the
far greater wrong of resenting it (Jesus never
resented anything or anyone — have we any
right to?). He may call us to be open with our
friends so that they may know us as we really
are, and thus be able to have genuine
fellowship with us. These acts may be
humiliating and a complete reversal of our
usual attitudes of pride and selfishness, but by
such acts we shall know true brokenness and
become partakers of the humility of the Lamb.
As we are willing to allow this to happen over

each issue, the blood of the Lamb will be able to cleanse us from all sin, and we shall walk with God dressed in white, with His peace in our hearts.

Notes
1. Colossians 1:20 2. Colossians 1:14; John 6:54
3. Revelation 12:11 4. 1 John 1:7 5. Hebrews 9:14
6. Hebrews 10:19 7. Revelation 7:14 8. John 1:29
9. Matthew 11:29 10. John 6:38 11. Philippians 2:8
12. Isaiah 53:7 13. Matthew 3:17 14. Philippians 2:5:
1 Corinthians 2:16 15. Matthew 5:23-24

To Think About

I need to be completely convinced about the power of the blood of Jesus. I must know that there is no sin from which it cannot cleanse and set me free. As I meditate on the following scriptures, may the Holy Spirit give me complete confidence in the power of the blood.

Colossians 1:19,20. For God was pleased to have all his fullness dwell in him, and through him to reconcile to himself all things, whether things on earth or things in heaven, by making peace through his blood, shed on the cross.

Revelation 12:11. They overcame him by the blood of the Lamb and by the word of their testimony; they did not love their lives so much as to shrink from death.

1 John 1:7. But if we walk in the light, as he is in the light, we have fellowship with one another, and the blood of Jesus, his Son, purifies us from all sin.

Hebrews 9:14. How much more, then, will the blood of Christ, who through the eternal Spirit offered himself unblemished to God, cleanse our consciences from acts that lead to death, so that we may serve the living God!

Hebrews 10:19-22. Therefore, brothers, since we have confidence to enter the Most Holy Place by the blood of Jesus, by a new and living way opened for us through the curtain, that is, his body, and since we have a great priest over the house of God, let us draw near to God with a sincere heart in full assurance of faith, having our hearts sprinkled to cleanse us from a guilty conscience and having our bodies washed with pure water.

10
PROTESTING OUR INNOCENCE?

We have all become so used to condemning the proud, self-righteous attitude of the Pharisee in the parable of the Pharisee and the Tax-collector[1], that we can hardly believe that the picture of him is meant to apply to us — which only shows how much like him we really are! How like the Pharisee the Sunday school teacher who finished her lesson on this parable with the words, 'And now, children, we can thank God that we are not the same as this Pharisee!' We are in most danger of adopting the Pharisee's attitude when God is wanting to humble us at the Cross of Jesus, and show us the sins in our hearts which are hindering personal revival.

God's picture of the human heart

We shall not understand the real wrong of the Pharisee's attitude, nor of our own, unless we view it against the background of what God says about the human heart. Jesus said, 'From within, out of men's hearts come evil thoughts, sexual immorality, theft, murder, adultery, greed, malice, deceit, lewdness, envy, slander, arrogance and folly.'[2] The same dark picture of the human heart is given to us in Paul's letter to the Galatians, 'The acts of the sinful nature are obvious; sexual immorality, impurity and debauchery; idolatry and witchcraft; hatred, discord, jealousy, fits of rage, selfish ambition, dissensions, factions and envy; drunkenness, orgies and the like.'[3] What a picture! Jeremiah makes the same point, 'The heart is deceitful above all things [that is, it deceives the man himself, so that he does not know himself], and beyond cure. Who can understand it?'[4]

Here, then, is God's picture of the human heart, the fallen self, the 'old self',[5] as the Scripture calls it, whether in the unconverted or in the keenest Christian. It is hard to believe that these things can proceed from the heart of ministers, evangelists, and Christian workers but they do. The simple truth is, that the only beautiful thing about the Christian is Jesus Christ. God wants us to recognise that fact as true in our experience, so that in true brokenness and self-despair we shall allow Jesus Christ to be our righteousness and holiness — our everything. That is victory.

Making God a liar!

Now in the face of God's description of the human heart we can see what it was that the Pharisee did. In saying, 'God, I thank you that I am not like other men — robbers, evil doers, adulterers', he was protesting his innocence of the very things that God says are in every heart. He said in effect, 'These things are doubtless true of other men — this Tax-collector is even now confessing them — but not of me, Lord!' And in so saying, he was making God a liar, for 'if we claim we have not sinned, we make Him out to be a liar,'[6] because He says we have! Yet I feel sure that he was perfectly sincere in what he said. He really *did* believe that he was innocent of these things. Indeed, he is attributing his imagined innocence to God, saying, 'I thank you...'. God's word, however, still stood against him, but he just had not seen it. The 'penny had not dropped'!

If the Tax-collector is beating upon his breast and confessing his sins, it is not because he has sinned more than the Pharisee. It is simply that the Tax-collector has seen that what God says, is woefully true of him, and the Pharisee has not. The Pharisee still thinks that outward abstinence from certain sins is all that God requires. He has not yet understood that God looks 'not at the outward appearance, but at the heart,'[7] and equates the look of lust with adultery[8], the attitude of resentment and hate with murder[9], considers envy as actual theft, and the petty tyrannies in the home as wicked as the most extortionate dealings in the market place.

How often have we, also, protested our innocence on the many occasions when God has been convicting others, and when He has wanted to convict us too. We have said in effect, 'These things may be true of others, but not of me!' and said so quite sincerely. Perhaps we have heard of others who have humbled themselves and have rather despised them for the confessions they have had to make and the things they have had to put right in their lives. Or perhaps we have been genuinely glad that they have been blessed. But, whichever, we do not feel that we have anything to be broken about ourselves.

My dear friend, if we feel we are innocent and have nothing to be broken about, it is not that these things are not there, but that we have not seen them. We have been deluding ourselves.

Unconscious sin separates us

God must be true in all that He says about us. In one form or another He sees these things expressing themselves in us (unless we have recognised them and allowed God to deal with them) — unconscious selfishness, pride, and self-congratulation; jealousy, resentment, and impatience; reserve, fears, and shyness; dishonesty and deception; impurity and lust; if not one thing, then another. But we are blind

to it. We are, perhaps, so occupied with the
wrong done to us, that we do not see that we
are sinning against Christ in not being willing
to accept it with His meekness and lowliness.
Whilst we see so clearly how the other person
wants his own way and his rights, we are blind
to the fact that we want ours just as much; and
yet we know there is something missing in our
lives. Somehow we are not in vital fellowship
with God. We have lost our spiritual cutting
edge. Unconscious sin is none the less sin with
God, and separates us from Him. The sin in
question may be quite a small thing which
God will readily show us, if we are only willing
to ask Him.

There is another error we fall into when we
are not willing to recognise the truth of what
God says about the human heart. Not only do
we protest our own innocence, but we often
protest the innocence of our loved ones. We
hate to see them being convicted and humbled
and we are quick to defend them. We do not
want them to confess anything. We are not
only living in a realm of illusion about
ourselves, but about them too, and we fear to
have it shattered. But it is from God that we
are trying to defend them — making God a
liar on their behalf, as we do on our own, and
preventing them from entering into blessing,
just as we prevent ourselves.

Only a deep hunger for real fellowship with
God will make us willing to cry to God for His
all-revealing light, and to obey it when
it is given.

God justified

This brings us to the Tax-collector. With all
that God says about the human heart in our
minds, we can see that his confession of sin
was simply a justification of God, an
admission that what God said of him was true.
Perhaps at one time he was like the Pharisee,
and did not believe that what God said about
man was really true of him. But the Holy
Spirit has shown him things in his life which
prove God right, and he is broken. Not only
does he prove God right in all that he has said,
but God is doubtlessly justified in all the
chastening judgements God has brought upon
him. Nehemiah's prayer might well have been
his, 'In all that has happened to us, you have
been just; you have acted faithfully, while we
did wrong.'[10]

This remains the nature of true confession
of sin, true brokenness. It is the confession
that my sin is not just a mistake, a slip,
something which is really foreign to my heart
('It is not like me to have such thoughts or do
such things!'). But that it is something which
reveals the real 'I'. It is something that shows
me to be the proud, rotten, unclean thing God
says I am, that it really *is* like me to have such
thoughts and do such things. It was in these
terms that David confessed his sin, when he
prayed, 'Against you, you only have I sinned
and done what is evil in your sight, *so that you
are proved right when you speak and justified
when you judge*.'[11] So let us not fear to make

such a confession when God convicts us that
we must, thinking it will 'let Jesus down.'
Rather the reverse is true, for out of such
confession God gets glory, for we declare Him
to be right. This brings us to a new experience
of victory in Christ, for it declares afresh, that
'nothing good lives in me, that is, in my sinful
nature',[12] and brings us to a place where we
give up trying to make our incorrigible selves
holy, and where we take Jesus to be our
holiness and His life to be our life.

Peace and cleansing

But the Tax-collector did something more than
prove God right. He pointed to the sacrifice
on the altar, and in doing so, found peace with
God and cleansing from sin. This comes out
in the literal meaning of the words which he
uttered, 'God, have mercy on me, a sinner.' In
the Greek, the words mean literally, 'God be
propitiated to me, the sinner.' The only way by
which a Jew knew that God could be
propitiated [appeased] was by a sacrifice, and
in all probability at that very hour the lamb for
the daily burnt offering was being offered up
on the altar in the temple.

It is the same with us. We never come to
this position of brokenness without God
showing us the divine Lamb on Calvary's
cross, cancelling our sins by the shedding of
His blood. The God who declares beforehand
what we are, provides beforehand for our sin.
Jesus was the Lamb slain for our sins from the

foundation of the world. In Him, who bore them in meekness, my sins are finished, and as I, in true brokenness, confess them, and put my faith in His blood, they are cleansed and gone. Peace with God then comes into my heart, fellowship with God is immediately restored, and I walk with Him dressed in white once more.

This simple way of being willing to declare God right and see the power of the blood to cleanse, brings within our reach, as never before, a close walk with Jesus; a constant dwelling with Him in the Most Holy Place. As we walk with Him in the light, He will be showing us all the time the beginning of things, which if allowed to continue, will grieve Him and check the flow of His life in us. Such things are the expression of that old, proud self, for which God has nothing but judgement.

At no point must we protest our innocence of what He shows us. All along we must be willing to declare, 'You are right, Lord; that just shows what I am,' and be willing to give it to Him for cleansing. As we do so, we shall find that His precious blood is continuously cleansing us from sin, and Jesus is able continuously to fill us with His Spirit. This demands that we must be people who are 'contrite and humble in spirit', willing to be shown the smallest thing. But such people, God says, 'live with Him in a high and holy place',[13] and experience continuous revival.

So this is our choice — to protest our

innocence and go home without God's blessing and out of touch with Him. Or to see God justified and to enter into peace, fellowship, and victory through the blood of Jesus.

Notes
1. Luke 18:9-14 2. Mark 7:21,22 3. Galatians 5:19-21
4. Jeremiah 17:9 5. Ephesians 4:22 6. 1 John 1:10
7. 1 Samuel 16:7 8. Matthew 5:27-28 9. 1 John 3:15
10. Nehemiah 9:33 11. Psalm 51:4 12. Romans 7:18
13. Isaiah 57:15

To Think About

How quickly I become like the Pharisee rather than the Tax-collector! But God is right, my heart is not pure and clean. When, for some time, I have not confessed my sin and am not aware of any conviction from the Holy Spirit, it is not because I am pure, but because I am blind and becoming hardened.

If that is the case, then I need to pray:

My Father in heaven, I do want close fellowship with you; so I confess that you are right and I am wrong. Without your conviction and cleansing, I will tend towards more and more wickedness and blindness. Please, show me my heart! Do not let my sins lie covered over by self-righteousness. Do not let me go on proclaiming my innocence, but show me my guilt. Thank you that the sacrifice of Jesus is sufficient for my sins and you will forgive me as I continue to acknowledge the seeds of wickedness in my heart.

As I have confessed my sins to you, Father, fill me with your Holy Spirit and draw me closer to you each day. I am willing to be shown the smallest sin that I may confess and be cleansed and so live my life full of the Spirit, in a state of continuing revival. Amen.

Personal notes

_____

_____

_____

11

FORTY YEARS ON —
A Personal Interview
with the Author

This chapter is a summary of three radio interviews with David Mains in the USA and broadcast in 1988 on 'The Chapel of the Air', Wheaton, Illinois.

What has been your experience of personal revival?

I am an evangelist, but above all I am concerned for the revival of the church, inasmuch as I had to have, and still have to have, a continuous experience of revival. At the beginning I had been working full-time as an evangelist — I had had some very fruitful years and many had turned to the Lord. Then, after a particular high peak, I found a decline set in and I somehow lost the power of the Holy Spirit and the liberty which I had once known in proclaiming the gospel. I tried to make up for the lack of power by my own efforts. I prayed longer; I studied harder; I preached more vehemently, but all to no avail: that lack persisted. I did not realise it at the

time, but that very state of decline was making
me a fit candidate for the grace of God. It was
Finney who said, 'Revival always presupposes
a declension[1]. Therefore if a man can't own up
to declension, he is no candidate for revival
personally.' Well, I was experiencing the
declension, but at that time was not willing to
admit it. At that point God sent back to
England some missionaries and African
leaders from Uganda, Rwanda and Kenya.
This was in 1947.

They came back from the revival in East
Africa, not merely to have a furlough, but to
share with us what they had been learning in
the revival. It had been going on for years.
These missionaries themselves were not the
fathers of the revival, rather some of its many
children. Very often they were brought into
the fullness of the blessing of the gospel of
Christ through the testimony and challenge of
the Africans. That revival was led more by the
Africans than by the missionaries.

I invited these men to be the speakers at my
conference, and had little idea that they would
be more concerned for the leader of that
conference than for anyone else. And they
really began to counsel me. They began to
share the little they had begun to see of my
need — and I was certainly in need! I was
experiencing a spiritual decline. One of them
said, 'Roy, you need to repent'. I said, 'Where
do I need to repent?' In all honesty I didn't
know — I was working so hard, I was praying
so much, I was preaching so fervently, doing

so much. They said, 'Well, we don't know where you need to repent. You see, we've only just got to know you. But we've got to know enough to be able to suggest at least one place where you might begin, and that's in your relationship with your wife. When we came to the campus, you said, 'Friends, get in the car, I've got to go to one of the other houses to make some arrangements.' And in that house we saw you talking to a young lady; we didn't know by the way you spoke to her whether she was your secretary or your wife. We suggest you might begin there, because revival for us began in our most intimate relationships — in the home.' I took this to heart. My message of 'victorious life' had ceased to work so I began to think I should forget it and see what light the Lord could give me for the present. That light came to show me sin where I hadn't seen it before, and I began on a path of repentance with my wife and in my attitude toward her. I was tense — and a tense man is a difficult person to live with. I had to see that things were not her fault but mine. I began to take them to Jesus and I, a well-known evangelist in England, began on a new path of repentance – calling sin *sin*. This in turn meant that I had to find a new power in the blood of Jesus Christ to deal with all the things that the light was revealing in my life.

You use the word 'brokenness'. You say that brokenness is always one of those first parts of revival. What do you mean by 'brokenness'?

This word occurs in several places in Scripture where the broken and the contrite heart is spoken of. But unless we really explain what we mean, that word could become a cliché. People might equate this with 'many tears' and 'terrible experiences.' It's nothing of the sort: it is a matter of the will. Brokenness is the opposite of hardness. Hardness says 'It's your fault,' brokenness says, 'It's mine.' It's a struggle for a person to be willing to say that, especially when he has expressed so loudly that he is right. When God wins a victory in his life he says, 'Friends *I'm* the one who is wrong.' They too may be wrong, but that's not his business. He is the one who's wrong and very often the wrong is his reaction to their wrong. They may be wrong in their actions, but he is wrong in his reactions — his anger, his resentment, his jealousy — and nothing is gained by confessing the other fellows' sins. It's got to be *me*, and brokenness is *me* being willing to do that.

Is brokenness something we take care of once and for all, or does brokenness remain a constant daily necessity?

It's a daily necessity, as the light continuously shows things up. The Word talks about walking in the light as He is in the light. Light is that which reveals, darkness that which hides. When the light of God shows up something that grieves Him, something wrong in me, my business is to say, 'Yes, Lord, You're right, I'm wrong' — and that's a daily thing. And as I do it, the blood of Jesus Christ is a daily cleansing for me.

In Chapter 1 you say, 'To be broken is the beginning of revival. It is painful, it is humiliating, but it is the only way . . . . It is being 'Not I but Christ,' and a 'C' is a bent 'I'.' What do you mean by that?

The concept of brokenness is set against the Scriptures that speak about the stiff neck. 'Do not be stiff-necked' comes in one or two places in the Old Testament. And when someone is accused, you can almost see his neck going stiff: 'That's not true, you're not right.' And you know, when at last he says, 'It's my fault', you can almost see the head bowed too. Those who came from East Africa came with a chorus one of them had written. These are the words:

Lord, bend that proud and stiff-necked I,
Help me to bow the head and die,
Beholding Him on Calvary,
Who bowed his head for me.

Chapter 2 is called 'Cups Running Over' and it is a word picture about new life in Christ. What do you mean by 'cups running over'?

'Cups running over' became a phrase during the revival in East Africa. It is, of course, taken from Psalm 23: 'My cup runneth over' (AV). It was used, and might still be used, to express the joy and the liberty that comes to a person who has been newly washed and made clean in the blood of Jesus Christ. It was first used by a dear friend of mine, Dr Joe Church. He was one of the early leaders of the revival and he gave a special picture at a great open-air conference in a natural amphitheatre. Thousands and thousands were there and he gave the picture of Jesus coming into that gathering with a golden water pot on His shoulder in which was the water of life. He suggested that if they needed to be filled with the Holy Spirit, they should hold out their hands in the shape of a cup. They should imagine that Jesus was coming down the rows with the golden water pot and filling their cup to overflowing with the water of life.

However, Jesus might come to some cup, look in, shake His head sadly and pass on by. That cup was stained and dirty and needed to be cleaned before it could be filled. Some people might say, 'This is not sin, it is just part of my make up.' Jesus replies, 'It is sin, and you must call it sin.' As you confess it, He cleanses the cup with His blood and fills it with the water of life. Hence the phrase, 'Cups running over'. When a man was newly cleansed he would say, 'Praise the Lord, my cup's now running over' — but only because the blood of Jesus had been applied.

Are you talking about big sins like murder, or adultery, or theft, or are you talking about everyday sins that would keep Christ from filling that cup?

Everyday sins, both big and small. There is no difference in God's sight. And many of them are not sins of action but sins of reaction. Maybe the wrong action was somebody else's, but my reaction to their action is wrong too. Jealousy, or anger, or resentment — that is enough to stain the cup and prevent Him from filling it. But if I confess those things as sin, the blood of Jesus Christ cleanses from all sin.

Do you think the average Christian today regularly does confess sin, or is this something that is somewhat foreign to Christian thinking?

Well, it was a bit foreign to my own thinking, even though I was an evangelist. I wouldn't have said at that time that repentance was an essential part of my Christian life. And for that reason the blood of Jesus Christ wasn't all that important to me. But now the blood of Jesus is all my hope and peace, all my righteousness. I have been helped to walk this way, calling things by their name and proving there is power, wonder-working power in the blood of Jesus Christ.

You talk about continuous revival. Now some people think of revival as happening at a point in time and then you can bask in the warmth of what took place. That's not what you're talking about, is it?

No, a thing that is in the past remains in the past, it is not affecting me in the present. But Jesus is alive in the present and His blood has never lost its power. The revival movement in Africa is the biggest demonstration of continuous revival. That revival is going on as never before; for one reason, because the blood has never lost its power and they on their part have been willing to go on repenting.

To use your word picture, I assume that you have held your cup up to Christ recently. When did you do this and how?

The Lord showed me recently something that I hadn't really seen as sin. Now that is the way God works. He shows you something to be sin that you hadn't considered to be sin. For the last few years I have been attending a local church without really appreciating it. I haven't really been *blessed* by it. I haven't enjoyed their style of singing. Oh, it's orthodox, and yet I could always find reasons for my failure to appreciate it. But the other day the Lord showed me, that at the bottom of it all was the fact that I had not been drawn into the church.

'You,' He said, 'have usually been out there at the front, but now you're just sitting in the pew.' Then some time later I was preparing a message on one of Jesus' parables — the one that says when you are invited to a feast, don't sit down in the highest place, but rather sit in the lowest place. The Lord said to me, 'You should have loved that lowest place, for there you would have found Me. I took the lowest place for you. But you have been restless because you've not been willing to accept it happily.' I confessed that sin and put it under the blood, and I found there was something new in my heart as a result. That has put me on the track of some other sins in my life, unsuspected forms of self — and every one of them is sin — but the blood of Jesus has never lost its power and is mighty enough, sufficient enough to bring even me into the fullness of the blessing of the gospel of Christ again.

Have you ever been in a situation where large numbers of people are experiencing revival, where many cups are overflowing?

Yes, but I hesitate to try and chalk up successes; that is one of the tendencies that I have to recognise as sin. If I dwell on it too much, it will be the end of the outpouring. I think one of the reasons people don't see success more often is that they are wanting it too much. It should be enough to have Jesus, and in Jesus all else. And He will take care of the outpouring to others.

Would you say that this topic of personal revival is a simple one?

It is certainly not complicated. We don't really need to introduce anything else other than is found in Scripture. 1 John 1:7 says, 'If we walk in the light, as he is in the light, we have fellowship with one another, and the blood of Jesus, his son, purifies us from all sin.' In John's writings light and darkness are not vague synonyms for good and evil. Light is simply that which reveals, darkness that which hides. God is light, the all-revealing one. If we are prepared to walk in His light and say yes to what his light may reveal as sin, we will remain in the light.

If God is to bless the reader through the pages of your book, you have said that he must come to them with a deep hunger of heart. He must be possessed with a dissatisfaction of the state of the church in general and of himself in particular — especially of himself. Now I've read that in a lot of other places. Why is it that revival so often begins with this sense of dissatisfaction?

Let's look at it like this: if you are going to enjoy the meal your wife has prepared for you, you've got to have a good appetite, you've got to be hungry. Perhaps you need to have a few unfortunate experiences of other people's cooking, and then you'll come back to the one whose cooking you know does satisfy. The same is true here: grace is flowing like a river,

millions of others have been supplied but
you've got to be hungry, *you've* got to be in
need. Such are the times in my life when I get
blessed. I do not get blessed when I read my
Bible as a matter of duty for a daily quiet time.
Rather, when I come feeling bad, those are the
times when it comes to life! Again and again I
have to say to the Lord, 'I want to tell You
something: I'm in poor shape spiritually.'

'Just fine,' says the Lord, 'anything else?'

'Well, I haven't got much peace.'

'Anything else? Come on, let it all out.'
When I come like that, grace meets me;
because when I admit that I'm in that position,
by the very nature of that admission I become
a candidate for that marvellous grace of our
loving Lord, grace that exceeds our sin and
our guilt. Grace is not God's reward for the
faithful, it's His gift for the empty, the feeble
and the failing. When I am feeling like that,
I'm the very one who is going to be blessed.

How would you explain grace to someone who doesn't know what it is?

Grace is the undeserved favour of God, and
no-one is a candidate for grace unless they are
undeserving. You can't be too down, too
wrong, for grace. That's where Jesus gets His
glory; not in the number of good Christians
He pats on the back, but in the failures He
restores.

You talk about the self-satisfied Pharisee and the dissatisfied Tax-collector in Chapter 10, 'Protesting our Innocence'?

We all naturally protest our innocence. We naturally justify ourselves; therefore we cannot be candidates for *God* to justify. God justifies the *un*godly. Have you ever heard a greater apparent contradiction? God who justifies the *un*godly! He who commands earthly judges 'You shall acquit the innocent and condemn the guilty'[2] is here doing the very opposite. 'I'm setting My court of grace — it's in order to justify those who are *un*godly.' He declares those to be right who admit they are wrong. To see that, gives you a bigger incentive than ever before to admit that very fact.

So all of self becomes a hindrance to revival? Whether it's selfishness, or self-effort; self-indulgence, self-pity or self-righteousness.

The things you've mentioned all begin with self. They are all sinful and it's not without significance that the central letter of the little word sin is 'I'.

It's a big problem to get beyond all that. Dissatisfaction — that's a good thing; when we are dissatisfied we aspire for something more, and God is able to satisfy. If we don't have any dissatisfaction we don't aspire for anything more.

I don't like the word 'aspire'; that looks as if I'm going to get better. I come empty; my dissatisfaction draws me to the One who has got something good for those who confess they are failures.

You use the word revival a lot but you don't equate that with an emotional high. Is revival ever emotional?

Of course. Life is full of emotion; it is sometimes sad, sometimes happy, sometimes exuberant. We're given good grounds for which to shout and praise; not that I'm wanting people to shout necessarily, but there is plenty of reason for it. When grace shows me that my righteousness is absolutely unassailable before God in the person of Jesus Christ, that I've boldness to enter the Holiest by the blood of Jesus, that I needn't go struggling and striving and mourning — that's something worth praising for! It isn't just an unaccountable emotion, that's the point. You're given solid rational grounds for your joy.

You come back to the blood of Jesus again and again. I am not sure the average person is conscious of the value of Christ's blood in terms of daily living. Do you sense Christ's blood being operative in your life on a daily basis?

Yes, but we need to define what we mean by the blood of Jesus. Some people are squeamish when they hear preaching about the blood. When they are asked to sing about the blood they lose their enthusiasm because some

people can't bear the sight of blood. The first
time a nurse is present at an operation she will
probably faint; and yet the Christian is always
boasting of the cross and of the blood of Jesus
Christ. So why do we do it? There is a
famous Old Testament incident, the Passover.
The first-born died in every house except
where that particular Jewish home had taken a
lamb, slain it, and sprinkled its blood upon the
door. Not only slain the lamb, but sprinkled
the blood, for God had said 'When I see the
blood I will pass over you.' Note that in the
instructions given for the slaying of the lamb
and the sprinkling of its blood these words
occur: 'the blood will be a sign for you.' A
sign of what? It was a sign of judgement met.
God said, 'Judgement is coming on every
house'; but the blood said, 'A lamb's been slain
here; the judgement that should have fallen on
the eldest son has fallen on the lamb, and it
can't come in a second time.' So the blood is a
sign of the fact that judgement has been met.
It's as simple as that; it always speaks of the
finished work of Christ.

There's a lovely hymn that we sing
sometimes:

> Jesus the sinner's friend
> We hide ourselves in Thee,
> God looks upon Thy sprinkled blood,
> It is our only plea.

The blood is a sign that all the judgement

that was *my* due has already been met and finished with.

Is that true in our lives on a daily basis?

Yes, indeed! There's the shedding of the blood once for all, but we've got to sprinkle it by faith, and claim it for everything that would otherwise put us out of fellowship with God.

This book was written in 1950. You were optimistic about what God was doing among His people then. Are you still optimistic about what God is doing?

I've been absolutely staggered by the way God has used the book. But it is not because of the book but the working of the Lord and the hunger of the saints of God. They are hungry as never before, and I want to spend my remaining days in helping to lead people back to Calvary, back to the blood, back to liberty, back to revival.

And the continuing popularity of the book is a good sign that people are still listening to this message, the message about Christ and His blood. Do you have any thoughts that can summarize what we've been saying about revival?

First it must begin with the individual; not with the other person, but with me. He may be wrong, but I'm wrong too, probably in my reactions to him. Therefore as far as I am concerned, it begins with me. Then secondly, I

think I need to repeat what Finney said:
'Revival always presupposes a declension.'
Therefore, in the nature of the case, the person
who is the most ready to admit there has been
a declension is the more likely to be a
candidate for revival. It's got to begin with the
admission of my need.

I would like to say very forcibly, revival is
not a green valley getting greener, but a valley
full of dry bones (Ezekiel 37) being made to
live again, and those bones to stand up to
become a mighty army. Not a good Christian
becoming a better Christian, but a man who is
prepared to confess 'Mine is a valley full of
dry bones' being made to live again.

I've heard people admit it and it's broken
their hearts. 'Mine is a valley of dry bones;
I'm a minister, maybe, but it's a valley full of
dry bones!' Splendid, brother; praise the Lord
that you were ready to confess it. If you but
realise it, that gives you your qualification for
Jesus.

He belongs to you if only by your failures;
Jesus is a specialist in sin. This is where He
excels. When you take that place, you're a
candidate *and you are not going to be
disappointed.*

Notes
1. declension: spiritual decline   2. Deuteronomy 25:1